the perfect party

RICK RODGERS

BIRTHDAY CELEBRATIONS

Surefire recipes and exciting menus for a flawless party!

ILLUSTRATIONS BY ROBBIN GOURLEY

WARNER TREASURES™
PUBLISHED BY WARNER BOOKS
A TIME WARNER COMPANY

Warner Treasures is a trademark of Warner Books, Inc.

Warner Books, Inc.
1271 Avenue of the Americas
New York, NY 10020

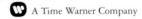 A Time Warner Company

Book design by Robbin Gourley
Printed in Singapore
First Printing: March 1996
10 9 8 7 6 5 4 3 2 1

ISBN: 0-446-91096-1

CONTENTS

INTRODUCTION

WHILE MOST OF THE IMPORTANT events in our lives are observed with feasts, the birthday dinner occupies a special position. It may be possible to get through Thanksgiving without a turkey, but I'm sure we all agree that a birthday isn't a birthday without the all-important birthday *cake*. Sure, we can all sing a chorus of "Happy Birthday," but unless the guest of honor's face is illuminated by candles on a cake, it just isn't right.

The practice of regularly celebrating birthdays wasn't established until around the fifth century, A.D. In antiquity, only the birthdays of royalty were commemorated, the pharaohs marking their annual natal celebrations with particular lavishness. The birth of Artemis, Greek goddess of the moon and the hunt, was celebrated with a honey cake, and may even have been topped with burning candles, which represented moonlight. Later, the birthdays of men of means were celebrated, but never common people, women, or children. When Christianity was established, birthday festivities were viewed as remnants of the pagan religions and therefore discouraged. By the fourth century, the Church had designated a date to mark the Nativity, December 25, and now that Christ's birth was celebrated, so too people slowly began having parties for their own birthdays.

Germany developed the ritual of the birthday cake as we know it today. In the thirteenth century, children's birthdays were celebrated for the first time, at a *Kinderfeste*, or "children's party." The day started with a cake topped with candles. The candles numbered one for each year of the child's age, and an extra one represented the "light of life." The candles were changed and kept burning throughout the entire day, which ended with a meal featuring the child's favorite foods. Then a secret wish was made and the candles were extinguished. Today, everyone enjoys these birthday traditions, not just children.

A child's birthday celebration is special, and that's why the first menu in this book is for a kid's birthday party. Since there likely will be adults at this party as well, the food has to satisfy both young and old. My trick is to make one basic dish and divide it into two portions—the one for kids stays mild in seasoning and I add a few extra ingredients to the other portion to make it more interesting for adults. Everyone loves an old-fashioned birthday cake with frosting, but the fun really gets going when you decorate the top with popular toys or dolls.

There's a real challenge in creating a birthday menu for teenagers. Adolescents may not know what they like, but they certainly tell you what they don't like. The solution is a big buffet where everyone can pick and choose. The food must also be fun, so I prepare a Tex-Mex buffet. Since some teenagers are vegetarians, or won't eat red meat, or don't like spicy foods, the buffet allows them to have anything from a big, fat burrito to a simple green salad.

A beautiful, elegantly prepared dinner is my favorite way to celebrate a friend's birthday. I pull out all the stops—the table is set with my best china and silver, and of course, beautiful flowers. The menu includes extra-special ingredients like wild mushrooms, a boned leg of lamb, chèvre, and carefully selected wines. Of course, an absolutely fabulous, knock 'em dead birthday cake must make an appearance, and it's a rare cake that can top my surefire White Chocolate Gift Box Cake.

These menus will inspire and help you prepare a perfect birthday party, no matter what the celebrant's age. Remember, one of the best gifts you can give a friend or loved one is your time. And the time you spend preparing a special meal in that friend's honor is a personal gift that is unsurpassable.

A KID'S BIRTHDAY PARTY

LOTS OF FRESH POPCORN
(GROWNUPS—SPICY CREOLE POPCORN)

BIG NOODLES WITH LITTLE MEATBALLS
(GROWNUPS—MEATBALL, MUSHROOM, AND RICOTTA
PASTA CASSEROLE)

GREEN SALAD WITH SALSA DRESSING

YOUR FAVORITE GARLIC BREAD*

Assorted Fruit Juices and Sodas

FAVORITE STUFF BIRTHDAY CAKE

For 12 children and 6 adults

*Recipe not included

W H E N I P R E P A R E A birthday party for a young friend, I often feel that I am having just as much fun as the young boy or girl. These events remind me of the joy I had at my own parties as a youngster. My mother is an exceptional baker, but she outdid herself creating birthday cakes that were truly works of art. Her first efforts were the "bunny with tinted coconut fur" variety, but as I grew older, and her expertise improved, she became renown for her superstructures of sweetness. For my sixteenth birthday, she created her *pièce de résistance:* a record player topped with a *faux* LP created from black-tinted frosting.

Menu planning for a youngster's birthday is simpler than creating a menu for adults because there are only so many foods that kids really enjoy. But that doesn't mean that adults at the party have to eat nursery food. The basic recipes here are made as two dishes, one for the kids and one for the grownups. The popcorn is served plain for the kids and with a garlic-and-spice butter for the adults. For the main course, the children will enjoy the amusing switch of Big Noodles with Little Meatballs, instead of the other way around. When you stir in sautéed mushrooms and ricotta cheese, adults have a hearty pasta casserole. (Both are placed into baking dishes, can be made well ahead of time, and baked just before serving.) Not many children relish green salads, but they are popular with adults. Just in case there are salad-loving kids in the group, I suggest a zesty, creamy Salsa Dressing that both young and old will enjoy. Since most parents discourage their kids from having too many sweets, there is nothing sugary served until cake time.

To close the party, an eye-catching birthday cake is the order of the day. Every child has his or her favorite things to collect; at the time of this writing, Power Rangers are it, just as Cabbage Patch Dolls were a few years ago. The Favorite Stuff Birthday Cake is an easy-to-make cake with a simple frosting that can be decorated with whatever figures delight the child. The decorations can be rinsed off and given as little presents to the birthday boy or girl, or as prizes for any games that will be played.

PREPARATION TIMETABLE

Up to 2 days ahead:
* Make tomato sauce for pasta; cool, cover, and refrigerate.
* Make Salsa Dressing.

Up to 1 day ahead:
* Make meatballs and finish sauce; cool, cover, and refrigerate.
* Make cake.
* Make frosting and frost cake; wrap in plastic wrap and refrigerate.

Up to 8 hours ahead:
* Prepare pasta.
* Finish kids' pasta; cover and refrigerate.
* Finish grownups' pasta; cover and refrigerate.
* Prepare lettuce and vegetables for salad; store in plastic bags and refrigerate.

Up to 4 hours ahead:
* Make popcorn; keep half plain for kids; store at room temperature.
* Make topping for Spicy Creole Popcorn; store at room temperature.

1 hour before serving:
* Remove cake from refrigerator.

45 minutes before serving:
* Bake pasta.

When ready to serve:
* Toss Spicy Creole Popcorn.
* Toss salad.

LOTS OF FRESH POPCORN GROWNUPS: SPICY CREOLE POPCORN

Makes about 4 quarts popped corn; 10 to 12 kid-size servings and 6 to 8 adult servings

For the kids, make the popcorn without butter and season with salt only, unless you want buttery handprints all over everything. The adults get a zippy garlic and spice seasoning that will make you wonder why more movie theaters don't serve popcorn this good. Make the popcorn by your favorite method: on top of the stove with oil or in a hot-air popping machine.

Spicy Creole Popcorn

4 tablespoons unsalted butter
2 large garlic cloves, crushed
2 tablespoons sweet paprika
1 teaspoon dried basil
1 teaspoon dried oregano
1 teaspoon salt
½ teaspoon onion powder
¼ teaspoon freshly ground pepper
⅛ teaspoon ground red (cayenne) pepper
16 cups popped popcorn (from about ¾ cup unpopped corn kernels)

Kids' Popcorn

8 cups popped popcorn (from about 6 tablespoons unpopped corn kernels)
Salt to taste

1. Make the kids' popcorn: Place popcorn in a large bowl and season with salt.

2. Make the Spicy Creole Popcorn: Heat butter and garlic in a small saucepan over medium-low heat until butter is melted. Continue cooking until garlic sizzles, about 1 minute. With a slotted spoon, lift out and discard garlic. In a small bowl, combine paprika, basil, oregano, salt, onion powder, and black and cayenne peppers. *The butter can be prepared up to 4 hours ahead of serving. Reheat over low heat before proceeding.*

3. Place popcorn in a very large bowl. While tossing, drizzle with butter mixture and toss until well coated. Sprinkle with spice mixture and toss again. Serve immediately, or at room temperature.

BIG NOODLES WITH LITTLE MEATBALLS GROWNUPS: MEATBALL, MUSHROOM, AND RICOTTA PASTA CASSEROLE

Makes two 3-quart casseroles; 10 to 12 kid-size servings and 6 adult servings

One big batch of pasta and meatballs in tomato sauce is easy to transform into two separate dishes, a plain one for kids and a gussied-up version for grownups. One important caveat about pasta preparation: do not crowd the pasta in the cooking water. If you don't have a pot large enough to handle two pounds of pasta at once, simply cook the pasta in two batches.

Tomato Sauce

2 tablespoons olive oil
1 large onion, chopped
2 garlic cloves, minced
2 (28-ounce) cans peeled tomatoes in juice, undrained, coarsely chopped
2 (8-ounce) cans tomato sauce
2 teaspoons dried basil
2 teaspoons dried oregano
1 bay leaf

Little Meatballs

$\frac{3}{4}$ cup dried bread crumbs
$\frac{1}{3}$ cup milk
2 large eggs, beaten
1 teaspoon salt
$\frac{1}{4}$ teaspoon freshly ground pepper
1 pound ground round beef (85 percent lean)
1 pound sweet Italian sausage, casings removed
1 medium onion, finely chopped
1 garlic clove, minced

2 pounds dried rigatoni
2 tablespoons olive oil
1 pound fresh mushrooms, sliced $\frac{1}{4}$ inch thick
1 (15-ounce) container part-skim ricotta cheese
1 (8-ounce) can tomato sauce
Freshly grated Parmesan cheese, for serving

1. Make the tomato sauce: In a large pot, heat oil over medium heat. Add onion and cook, stirring often, until softened, about 5 minutes. Add garlic and stir for 1 minute. Add tomatoes with their juice, tomato sauce, basil, oregano, and bay leaf. Bring to a simmer. Reduce heat to low and simmer until slightly thickened, about 1 hour. *The sauce can be prepared up to 2 days ahead of serving, cooled, covered, and refrigerated. Reheat to simmering over low heat in the same pot before proceeding.*

2. Make the meatballs: In a large bowl, mix the bread crumbs, milk, eggs, salt, and pepper. Add the ground beef, sausage, onion, and garlic and mix well until blended. Using a heaping teaspoon for each, form mixture into small meatballs and place on a baking sheet. *Meatballs can be prepared up to this point 8 hours ahead, covered, and refrigerated.*

3. One at a time, quickly drop the meatballs into the simmering sauce, stirring gently a few times during the additions to be sure all of the meatballs are coated with sauce. Cook until the meatballs are firm and cooked through, about 20 minutes. Skim off any fat that rises to the surface. *The meatball sauce can be prepared up to 1 day ahead, cooled completely, covered, and refrigerated.*

4. In a very large pot, bring 8 quarts of water to a boil and add 2 tablespoons of salt. Add the rigatoni and cook until barely tender, about 9 minutes. Do not overcook the pasta—it will cook further in the oven. Drain well.

5. Return the pasta to the pot and mix well with the meatball sauce. Transfer to 2 lightly oiled 10-by-15-inch glass baking dishes. *The casseroles can be prepared up to 8 hours ahead, covered, and refrigerated.*

6. In a large skillet, heat oil over medium heat. Add mushrooms and cook, stirring occasionally, until they give off their juices, liquid evaporates, and mushrooms begin to brown, about 8 minutes. *The mushrooms can be prepared up to 1 day ahead, covered, and refrigerated.*

7. When ready to serve, preheat the oven to 350°F. Stir the mushrooms and the ricotta cheese into one of the casseroles; this is the grownups' dish. Stir the tomato sauce into the other casserole; this is the kids' dish. Cover both casseroles with foil. Bake until heated through, about 45 minutes. Serve hot, with Parmesan cheese on the side for sprinkling.

GREEN SALAD WITH SALSA DRESSING

Makes 10 to 12 kid-size servings and 6 adult servings

Use your favorite prepared salsa from the supermarket, but choose a mild version so the kids' tender taste buds won't be offended.

Salsa Dressing

$\frac{1}{2}$ cup sour cream
$\frac{1}{2}$ cup mayonnaise
$\frac{3}{4}$ cup prepared salsa

Green Salad

2 medium heads green lettuce, rinsed and torn into bite-size pieces
2 pints cherry tomatoes, halved
1 medium cucumber, peeled and sliced
1 medium carrot, shredded
1 medium celery, cut crosswise into $\frac{1}{4}$-inch-thick slices

1. Make the salsa dressing: In a medium bowl, stir sour cream, mayonnaise and salsa. *The dressing can be prepared up to 2 days ahead, covered, and refrigerated.*

2. Before serving, toss lettuce, tomatoes, cucumber, carrot, and celery with dressing. Serve chilled.

FAVORITE STUFF
BIRTHDAY CAKE

Makes 12 to 18 servings

When I recently made this cake for a young friend, he requested a dinosaur motif. I had a lot of fun at toy stores looking for inexpensive plastic monsters to adorn the cake. While shopping, I also found some plastic palm trees and even some candies decorated to look like rocks. This recipe makes a large rectangular vanilla-flavored cake. If your family prefers chocolate, see the notes at the end of the recipe to make the switch easily.

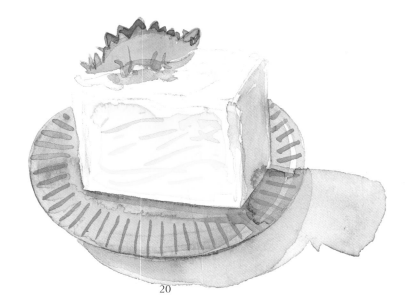

Cake

2½ cups cake flour (not self-rising)
1 tablespoon baking powder
¼ teaspoon salt
12 tablespoons (1½ sticks) unsalted butter,
    at room temperature
1½ cups granulated sugar
3 large eggs, at room temperature
1 teaspoon vanilla extract
¾ cup milk, at room temperature

Frosting

10 tablespoons (1¼ sticks) unsalted butter,
    at room temperature
5 cups confectioners' sugar, sifted
1 teaspoon vanilla extract
5 tablespoons milk, approximately
Paste or liquid food coloring (see Note), as
    needed

Small toys (dinosaurs, Power Rangers,
    dolls, trucks, airplanes, horses) and
    candy for decorations

1. Make the cake: Preheat oven to 350°F. Line the bottom of a 9-by-13-inch baking pan with waxed paper. Butter and flour inside of pan, tapping out excess flour.

2. Sift flour, baking powder, and salt onto a piece of waxed paper; set aside.

3. In a medium bowl, using a hand-held electric mixer at high speed, beat butter until smooth, about 1 minute. Add sugar and continue beating until light in color, about 2 minutes. Beat in eggs, one at a time, then vanilla. Alternating in thirds, beat in the flour mixture and milk, scraping sides of bowl often with a rubber spatula. Scrape into prepared pan and smooth the top.

4. Bake until a toothpick inserted in center of cake comes out clean, 30 to 35 minutes. Cool cake in pan on wire cake rack for 10 minutes. Run a sharp knife around inside of pan to release cake. Invert onto rack and unmold. Carefully peel off waxed paper. Cool completely. *The cake can be made 1 day ahead, wrapped in plastic wrap, and stored at room temperature.*

5. Make the frosting: In a medium bowl, using an electric mixer, beat butter until smooth. Gradually beat in confectioners' sugar. Beat in vanilla, and then enough of the milk to make a smooth, spreadable frosting. To make frosting for writing the inscription, transfer ½ cup of frosting to a small bowl. Stir in drops of food coloring to reach the desired color (see Note). Place the frosting in a pastry bag fitted with a small writing tip, such as Ateco number 5.

6. Place cake on a serving platter. Using a metal spatula, spread top and sides of cake with plain frosting. Using colored frosting in pastry bag, write inscription on cake, allowing room for the decorations. *The cake can be prepared up to 1 day ahead, covered loosely with plastic wrap—insert toothpicks into cake to keep plastic wrap from touching inscription—and stored at cool room temperature. If the cake is refrigerated, let stand at room temperature for 1 hour before serving.*

7. Whenever convenient before serving, decorate cake as desired with plastic toys and candies. Remove toys and other inedible objects from frosting before serving.

Chocolate Cake: sift ⅓ cup Dutch-process cocoa powder (such as Dröste) with the dry ingredients. For a chocolate frosting, add 3 tablespoons cocoa powder with the confectioners' sugar.

Note: While liquid food coloring is easily available at supermarkets, many specialty kitchenware and food shops sell paste food coloring. Paste food coloring will give richer, darker colors. Dip a toothpick into the paste color to transfer it in very small portions to the bowl of uncolored frosting.

A TEENAGER'S BURRITO BUFFET BIRTHDAY BASH

CHILE CON QUESO Y CARNE DIP

TORTILLA CHIPS*

CHICKEN BURRITO FILLING

YELLOW MEXICAN RICE

REFRIED BEANS

SHREDDED LETTUCE

TOMATO SALSA*

SHREDDED CHEDDAR CHEESE

FLOUR TORTILLAS

CITRUS VINAIGRETTE AND EASY RANCH DRESSING

Assorted Juices and Sodas

CHOCOLATE BROWNIE PIZZA

For 12 people

*Store-bought; no recipe given

WHEN GIVING A PARTY for a teenager, it's a good idea for the adults to stay out of the picture as much as possible. Adults will probably want to be in the same house to keep an eye on things, but this menu is designed to let you set everything up on a table, then get *out.*

Rather than make the party an entirely at-home event, tie it into some kind of outside activity and serve the meal at the start or finish of the occasion. During the afternoon, take them rollerblading, or to a movie, and let them come back to the buffet, cake, and gift opening. Or invite the guests over early in the evening for supper before dropping them off someplace off-premises (perhaps at a skating rink or sports center). In my area, there are a number of stores that carry inexpensive international tableware and trinkets, and at your local version you will be able to find some interesting decorations for your table. Party supply shops can also be helpful. Look in the Yellow Pages for Hispanic grocery stores, as sometimes they carry Mexican souvenirs as well as food. I put the tortilla chips in the brim of an inexpensive straw sombrero and use a burro-shaped piñata as a centerpiece and a vibrant serape as a tablecloth for this party.

It is impossible to guess the exact food preferences for a group of teenagers, so I put out a huge spread as a burrito-making buffet. A cheesey, beefy Chile con Queso y Carne Dip with tortilla chips is always fun to eat and sets the mood for the Tex-Mex fare to follow. The buffet is centered around a Chicken Burrito Filling, as practically all teenagers like poultry. They can add Yellow Mexican Rice, Refried Beans, Shredded Lettuce and Salsa (just buy two or three jars of your favorite brand, as a homemade version would probably not be as popular as the store-bought) as they wish. Put out a bowl of one pound of shredded cheddar cheese. Thinly slice 2 heads of iceberg lettuce to yield 12 cups—this amount will be enough to fill burritos and do double-duty as a salad. Offer the guests a choice of either slightly sweet Citrus Vinaigrette or Easy Ranch Dressing to put on the lettuce, if they want to create a salad. Teenagers love to be *blasé,* but the Chocolate Brownie Pizza should get their attention.

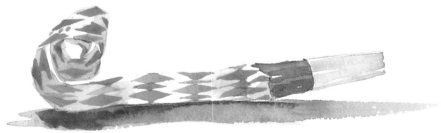

PREPARATION TIMETABLE

Up to 3 days ahead:
★ Make Citrus Vinaigrette; cover and refrigerate.
★ Make Easy Ranch Dressing; cover and refrigerate.

Up to 2 days ahead:
★ Make base for Chile con Queso y Carne Dip; cool, cover, and refrigerate.
★ Make Refried Beans; cool, cover, and refrigerate.

Up to 1 day ahead:
★ Prepare Chicken Burrito Filling; cool, cover, and refrigerate.
★ Shred lettuce and cheese; store in plastic bags and refrigerate.
★ Make Chocolate Pizza Brownie; cover with plastic wrap and store at room temperature.

45 minutes before serving:
★ Prepare Yellow Mexican Rice;

cover tightly and store in a warm place to keep warm.

30 minutes before serving:
★ Add cheese to dip base; transfer to serving dish.

15 minutes before serving:
★ Heat flour tortillas.

Just before serving:
★ Reheat Chicken Burrito Filling; transfer to serving dish.

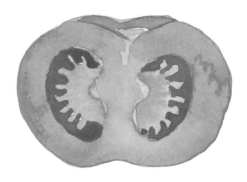

CHILE CON QUESO Y CARNE DIP

Makes 12 servings

Get out the fondue pot, chafing dish, or mini slow-cooker to keep this dish warm while serving. I find most teenagers prefer mildly spiced foods, so I opt for the less spicy supermarket canned chiles. However, you can use a fresh jalapeño pepper, seeded and minced.

12 ounces ground round beef (85 percent lean) or ground turkey
1 small onion, finely chopped
3 tablespoons chopped canned green chiles, drained and rinsed
1 garlic clove, minced
$\frac{1}{4}$ teaspoon salt
$\frac{1}{8}$ teaspoon ground red (cayenne) pepper
$\frac{1}{2}$ cup chopped and drained canned peeled tomatoes
2 tablespoons all-purpose flour
$\frac{3}{4}$ cup milk
$1\frac{1}{2}$ cups (6 ounces) shredded sharp cheddar cheese
$1\frac{1}{2}$ cups (6 ounces) shredded Monterey jack cheese
Tortilla chips, for serving

1. In a large nonstick skillet, cook ground meat, onion, chiles, garlic, salt, and cayenne pepper over medium-high heat, stirring often to break up meat with a spoon, until meat loses its pink color, about 6 minutes.

Drain off all fat. Stir in tomatoes and cool until tomato juices evaporate, about 2 minutes. Sprinkle with flour and stir for 1 minute. Pour in milk and bring to a simmer, stirring. Reduce heat to low and cook until thickened, about 1 minute. *The dip can be made to this point up to 2 days before serving. Reheat in a double boiler over boiling water, stirring often.*

2. Gradually add cheeses to hot beef mixture, stirring to melt each addition before adding another. Transfer to an electric mini slow-cooker, fondue pot, or chafing dish to keep warm while serving with tortilla chips for dipping.

CHICKEN BURRITO FILLING

M a k e s   a b o u t   6   c u p s

A wonderful bonus of this recipe is the homemade chicken stock it produces. Save it for reheating the chicken and making the Yellow Mexican Rice on page 33. Be sure to freeze any leftovers for other dishes.

2 (4-pound) chickens, cut into 8 pieces
1 large onion, sliced
2 garlic cloves, crushed
1 teaspoon salt
$\frac{1}{4}$ teaspoon peppercorns

1. In a large pot, place chickens, onion, and garlic. Add enough cold water to cover by 1 inch. Bring to a simmer over high heat, skimming off any foam that rises to surface. Add salt and peppercorns. Reduce heat to low and simmer until the chicken is almost tender when pierced with

the tip of a knife, about 30 minutes. Remove from heat, cover, and let stand for 1 hour, until chicken is completely cooked. (Cut into a drumstick at the bone, and if any trace of red remains, bring the chicken back to a boil and cook for 5 more minutes. Cool uncovered.)

2. Strain the broth into a large bowl and reserve. Let chicken cool until easy to handle. Remove and discard skin and bones. Using your fingers, pull and shred chicken meat. Trans-

fer to a large plastic bag with a zipper closure. Pour in 1 cup of the reserved broth. Close and refrigerate until ready to serve. *The chicken can be prepared up to 1 day before serving, cooled, covered, and refrigerated.*

3. To serve, place chicken and broth in a large saucepan. Heat over medium-low heat, stirring often, until heated through, about 7 minutes. Transfer to a chafing dish or heated serving bowl placed on an electric hot plate and serve hot.

YELLOW MEXICAN RICE
M a k e s   8   c u p s

The yellow and red colors in this tasty dish add a bright touch to the buffet. You may want to keep this recipe around to serve as a side dish for family meals—it is easily halved for a smaller quantity.

2 tablespoons olive oil
1 large onion, chopped
1 medium red bell pepper, seeded and
   chopped
2 garlic cloves, minced
2 cups long-grain rice
1 teaspoon turmeric
1 teaspoon ground cumin
1 teaspoon salt
$\frac{1}{4}$ teaspoon freshly ground pepper
4 cups chicken stock, preferably homemade
   from Chicken Burrito Filling (pages
   31–32)

1. In a large saucepan, heat oil over medium heat. Add onion, red pepper, and garlic. Cook, stirring often, until softened, about 6 minutes. Add rice and stir until evenly opaque white, about 1 minute. Stir in turmeric, cumin, salt, and pepper. Add broth and bring to a simmer.

2. Reduce heat to low. Cover tightly and cook until rice is tender, about 20 minutes. Let stand for 5 minutes. Fluff with a fork and transfer to a warmed serving bowl and serve hot. Covered tightly and kept in a warm place, the rice will stay warm for about 30 minutes. *Rice is always best when freshly made, but it can be prepared up to 1 day ahead, cooled, covered, and refrigerated. Chilled rice can be reheated in a large nonstick skillet, like Asian fried rice. Heat 2 tablespoons of olive oil over medium heat. Add the rice and cook, stirring often, until heated through, about 5 minutes.*

REFRIED BEANS

Makes 12 servings

Overachievers may wish to prepare the pinto beans from scratch—be my guest. But for a teenager's get-together, the guests will probably not appreciate your effort.

1 tablespoon vegetable oil
5 ounces bacon, coarsely chopped
1 large onion, chopped
3 garlic cloves, minced
1 teaspoon dried oregano
$\frac{1}{2}$ teaspoon ground cumin
$\frac{1}{8}$ teaspoon ground red (cayenne) pepper
5 (15-ounce) cans pinto beans, drained, reserving 1 cup liquid; or 6 cups freshly cooked beans and 1 cup reserved cooking liquid

1. In a medium nonstick skillet, heat the oil over medium heat. Add the bacon and cook, stirring often, until the bacon is browned and crisp, about 4 minutes. Using a slotted spoon, transfer the bacon to paper towels to drain, leaving fat in skillet.

2. Add onion and garlic to skillet. Cook, stirring often, until onion is softened, about 5 minutes. Stir in the oregano, cumin, and red pepper. Reduce heat to low. In batches, add the pinto beans. Using a large wooden spoon, mash the beans in the skillet as you add them, gradually

34

adding the reserved bean liquid as you mash. Mash and cook until heated through and almost smooth with a few chunks of beans remaining, about 8 minutes total. Stir in reserved bacon. Transfer to a warmed serving bowl and serve hot. *The beans can be prepared up to 2 days before serving. To reheat, heat 2 tablespoons of oil in a large nonstick skillet over medium heat. Add the mashed beans and cook, stirring often, until heated through, about 5 minutes.*

FLOUR TORTILLAS

M a k e s   1 2   t o r t i l l a s

Large flour tortillas made just for homemade burritos are now available at supermarkets. They are easy to heat up in a regular oven, but if you have a large microwave oven, you can follow the instructions on the package.

12 (11-inch) flour tortillas

1. Preheat the oven to 350°F. Stack tortillas, sprinkling each with a few drops of water. Wrap the stack in aluminum foil.

2. Bake until heated through, 10 to 15 minutes. Unwrap and serve hot, wrapped in a napkin to keep warm.

CITRUS VINAIGRETTE

Makes about 2 ¼ cups

Orange juice adds a slightly sweet note to a salad dressing that may become a regular family favorite. By making it in the blender, the mixture will emulsify better, and stay thick for easier serving at the buffet.

½ cup orange juice
2 tablespoons balsamic vinegar
2 tablespoons red wine vinegar
2 tablespoons sugar
1 tablespoon Dijon mustard
1 teaspoon salt
½ teaspoon freshly ground pepper
1½ cups olive oil

1. In a blender, process all the ingredients except the oil. With the machine running, gradually add the oil through the feed hole in the blender's top and process until smooth. *The dressing can be prepared up to 3 days ahead, covered, and refrigerated. If necessary, shake well to blend.*

2. For serving, transfer dressing to a small pitcher or a bowl with a small ladle, and let each guest use the amount desired.

EASY RANCH DRESSING

Makes about 2 ½ cups

Thick, rich, and creamy dressings go over big with teens. This is one of the best, but just don't tell them it has buttermilk in it.

1 cup mayonnaise
1 cup buttermilk
¼ cup minced celery with leaves
1 small onion, grated
1 teaspoon celery salt
½ teaspoon freshly ground pepper

1. In a medium bowl, whisk together all of the ingredients until blended. *The dressing can be prepared up to 3 days ahead, covered, and refrigerated. If necessary, shake well to blend.*

2. For serving, transfer dressing to a small pitcher or a bowl with a small ladle, and let each guest use the amount desired.

CHOCOLATE BROWNIE PIZZA

Makes 12 to 16 servings

A 12-inch deep-dish pizza pan, available at most kitchenware stores, is needed for this dessert. Look for a large chunk of white chocolate, rather than thin bars; it will shred more easily to make the "melted mozzarella" topping.

1 cup (4 ounces) pecans
1 cup (2 sticks) unsalted butter
6 ounces unsweetened chocolate, finely chopped
4 large eggs, at room temperature
2 cups packed light brown sugar
2 teaspoons vanilla extract
$\frac{3}{4}$ cup all-purpose flour
$\frac{1}{2}$ teaspoon salt
1 cup colored, sugar-coated chocolate candies (such as M & M's)
A 4- to 6-ounce chunk white chocolate

1. Preheat the oven to 350°F. Lightly butter and flour a 12-by-1-inch round deep-dish pizza pan.

2. Place pecans on a baking sheet and bake, tossing occasionally, until lightly toasted, about 10 minutes. Cool completely and coarsely chop.

3. In a medium saucepan, melt butter over medium heat. Remove from heat and sprinkle in chocolate. Let stand for 2 minutes, then whisk until smooth. Let stand until tepid, about 10 minutes.

4. In a medium bowl, using a hand-held electric mixer set at high speed, beat eggs and brown sugar until light in color and texture, about 2 minutes. Beat in tepid chocolate mixture and vanilla. Using a wooden spoon, stir in flour and salt. Stir

in the cooled pecans. Transfer to prepared pan and spread evenly.

5. Bake for 15 minutes. Gently pull the oven rack with the pizza pan on it a few inches out of the oven. Sprinkle colored candies over top of the brownie, and slide the rack back into oven. Continue baking until a toothpick inserted inches from center of brownie comes out with a moist crumb, about 20 minutes. Transfer to a wire rack.

6. Using the coarse holes on a cheese grater, shred white chocolate from the chunk over top of brownie. (You will use only about 2 ounces, but it is easier to grate this amount from a large chunk.) Cool brownie completely before serving directly from the pan. *The brownie can be prepared up to 1 day ahead, covered tightly with plastic wrap, and stored in the pan at room temperature.*

AN ELEGANT BIRTHDAY DINNER

CHÈVRE-PESTO CHEESECAKE WITH BAGUETTE TOASTS

Champagne

THREE-MUSHROOM SOUP WITH PORT AND TARRAGON

BAKERY FRENCH ROLLS*

Sauvignon Blanc

LAMB STUFFED WITH ROASTED GARLIC AND SPINACH

MEDITERRANEAN VEGETABLE AND POTATO GRATIN

Cabernet Sauvignon

WHITE CHOCOLATE GIFT BOX CAKE

Freshly Brewed Coffee and Tea

Assorted After-Dinner Cognacs and Liqueurs

For 8 people

*Recipe not included

ONE OF THE EASIEST ways to celebrate a friend's birth-day is to make a reservation at a popular restaurant and treat the guest to a nice dinner. Easy, yes, but not exactly personal. To my taste, serving a special dinner at home is much more pleasant. Even though I am doing the cooking, I am more relaxed serving dinner at home because I am in control of the setting, from music to lighting. My self-assured feeling is helped by the menu, which was carefully chosen for its ease of preparation.

This menu is one that you could find at an excellent French bistro. French cuisine always adds a certain *je ne sais quoi,* yet many of its signature dishes can be made well ahead. This is not to say that this is peasant food, as I have included some pricier ingredients that we save for special occasions. I begin with a savory Chèvre-Pesto Cheesecake that is perfect with a chilled apéritif or Champagne. *Cheesecake* brings dessert to mind, but just think of this as a tangy molded spread.

Soup is always my first choice to start a sit-down dinner, as it takes a minimum amount of effort to reheat and serve. Three-Mushroom Soup with Port and Tarragon is a lovely opener, and can be served with a smooth Sauvignon Blanc or the same red wine as with the meat.

Now that your guests' appetites have been well whetted, serve the main course, a luxurious Lamb Stuffed with Roasted Garlic and Spinach. While I find my friends say they don't eat as much red meat as they used to, a glorious roast becomes one of the occasions where they indulge. When I first started cooking, the number of side dishes and sauces you prepared for a main course was an indication of your proficiency as a cook. Thank goodness those days are over! I roast an uncomplicated Mediterranean Vegetable and Potato Gratin that not only bursts with flavor but combines the vegetable and starch courses. This entree calls for the best Cabernet Sauvignon or Bordeux you can find. If you wish to extend the time you spend around the dining table, serve a green salad. I don't find it a necessity, but if you are a salad lover, try the Citrus Vinaigrette on page 36 with romaine lettuce and grapefruit sections.

This meal deserves an extraordinary finish, supplied by the White Chocolate Gift Box Cake. It has a stunning appearance that will have your friends believing you purchased it at the finest *chocolatier-patisserie* in town. To serve with the cake, I buy the best coffee available, usually in a decaffeinated, flavored variety—the aroma of freshly brewed hazelnut or almond coffee always gets a favorable response from my guests.

When having friends over for a fancy dinner, also spend time attending to the details surrounding the meal. As always, set the table well ahead of time, putting out the serving dishes and utensils as well. Polish the silver and wash the crystal a day ahead, as that is a time-consuming chore that will cause much consternation if delayed. Don't forget to put candles on the grocery list—dripless ones—or opt for votive candles. In addition to flowers for the dining table (not too tall!), make a small arrangement for the coffee table or where the appetizer and drinks will be served. Place a rose or tulip in a bud vase along with a scented candle in the bathroom.

Remember, you want to spend time with your friends, not in the kitchen. This menu will keep you out of the kitchen as much as possible, allowing you to be so collected during the party that your friends may think it was catered. *Bon appétit, et Joyeux Anniversaire.*

PREPARATION TIMETABLE

Up to 3 days ahead:
* Make the cheesecake but do not add pesto topping; cool, cover, and refrigerate.
* Make chocolate cake layers; cool, wrap tightly in plastic wrap, and store at room temperature.
* Make raspberry syrup; cover and refrigerate.

Up to 2 days ahead:
* Make Three Mushroom Soup; cool, cover, and refrigerate.

Up to 1 day ahead:
* Set table (without flowers).
* Make the lamb sauce base; cool, cover, and refrigerate.
* Make lamb stuffing (without eggs); cool, cover, and refrigerate.
* Make chocolate ribbons (allow about 2 hours for ribbon paste to firm before rolling out).

* Make white chocolate frosting.
* Frost and finish White Chocolate Gift Box Cake; wrap in plastic wrap and refrigerate.

Up to 8 hours ahead:
* Make Baguette Toasts; store in a plastic bag at room temperature.

Up to 4 hours ahead:
* Add eggs to stuffing; stuff lamb; cover and refrigerate.
* Prepare gratin without potatoes; cover tightly and store at room temperature.

About 2 hours before serving dinner:
* Roast lamb.
* Add potatoes to gratin; bake.

Just before guests arrive:
* Spread pesto over cheesecake.

Just before serving dinner:
* Reheat soup.

* Remove lamb from oven, transfer to carving platter, and let stand in a warm place.
* Make lamb sauce; keep warm.

CHÈVRE-PESTO CHEESECAKE WITH BAGUETTE TOASTS

Makes 8 to 12 servings

Here's a savory appetizer to spread on toasted baguette slices and enjoy with predinner drinks. Whenever I serve this, I spread a few toasts with the cheesecake and place them on the platter to avoid confusion as to how to serve.

1 tablespoon unsalted butter, softened

1½ tablespoons dried bread crumbs

12 ounces rindless goat cheese (chèvre), such as Bucheron or Montrachet, at room temperature

2 large eggs, at room temperature

12 ounces cream cheese, at room temperature

½ cup sour cream

1 tablespoon cornstarch

¼ teaspoon salt

¼ teaspoon freshly ground pepper

1 loaf French or Italian bread, sliced ¼ inch thick

¼ cup extra-virgin olive oil

1 cup pesto, homemade or store-bought

1. Preheat oven to 300°F. Using a paper towel, coat the inside of an 8-inch springform pan with the butter. Sprinkle with bread crumbs, turning to coat with the crumbs. Wrap the outside bottom of pan tightly with aluminum foil.

2. In a large bowl, using a handheld electric mixer at medium speed, beat goat cheese with eggs until smooth. Gradually beat in cream cheese, beating until smooth again. Beat in sour cream, cornstarch, salt, and pepper. Spread evenly in the prepared pan. Place springform pan in a large baking pan and add enough hot water to come 1 inch up sides.

3. Bake until cheesecake is lightly puffed and seems set in the center, about 1 hour. Remove springform pan from water. Run a sharp knife around edges of pan to release cake. Cool completely on a wire cake rack. Remove sides of pan and wrap tightly in plastic wrap. Chill at least 4 hours or overnight. *The cheesecake can be prepared to this point up to 3 days ahead, covered, and refrigerated.*

4. Meanwhile, increase oven temperature to 400°F. Place bread slices on baking sheets and brush with olive oil. Bake until lightly browned and crisp, about 10 minutes. Cool completely. *The toasts can be prepared up to 8 hours ahead and stored in plastic bags at room temperature.*

5. When ready to serve, transfer cheesecake to a serving platter. Spread top with pesto, allowing excess pesto to run down sides. Arrange toasts around cheesecake. Let stand at room temperature for about 1 hour before serving. Allow guests to serve themselves, spreading a bit of pesto-topped cheesecake on a toast.

THREE-MUSHROOM SOUP WITH PORT AND TARRAGON

Makes 8 servings

An elegant trio of fresh button and shiitake mushrooms with dried porcini mushrooms makes a sophisticated make-ahead first course. Porcini mushrooms have a full, earthy flavor and are available at many specialty food stores. (The French call these *cèpes*.) If you can't find them, use Polish dried black mushrooms from the supermarket.

1 cup boiling water

1 cup (1 ounce) dried porcini mushrooms, rinsed in cold water to remove grit

2 tablespoons unsalted butter

2 medium leeks, white part only, well rinsed and finely chopped

12 ounces fresh shiitake mushrooms, stems discarded, caps sliced into $\frac{1}{4}$-inch-thick strips

10 ounces fresh button mushrooms, sliced $\frac{1}{4}$ inch thick

$\frac{1}{4}$ cup vintage or tawny port

1 teaspoon dried tarragon

$\frac{1}{3}$ cup all-purpose flour

$5\frac{1}{2}$ cups chicken stock, preferably homemade, or use low-sodium canned broth

$\frac{1}{2}$ teaspoon salt

$\frac{1}{4}$ teaspoon freshly ground pepper

$\frac{1}{2}$ cup sour cream, at room temperature, for garnish

2 tablespoons chopped fresh parsley, for garnish

1. In a small bowl, pour boiling water over porcini; let stand until mushrooms are softened, about 30 minutes. Lift out mushrooms and chop coarsely; set aside. Pour soaking liquid through a cheesecloth-lined strainer into a bowl and set aside.

2. In a soup pot, melt butter over medium heat. Add leeks and cook, stirring often, until softened, about 5 minutes. Increase heat to medium-high and add shiitakes, fresh button mushrooms, and the chopped porcini. Cook, stirring often, until mushrooms have given off their liquid, it evaporates, and mushrooms begin to brown, about 7 minutes. Add port and tarragon and boil until port is almost evaporated, about 2 minutes.

3. Reduce heat to medium, sprinkle flour over mixture and stir for

1 minute. Stir in mushroom soaking liquid, stock, salt, and pepper, scraping up any flour on bottom of pot with a wooden spoon. Bring to a simmer and cook, partially covered, for 10 minutes. *The soup can be prepared up to 2 days ahead, cooled, covered, and refrigerated. Reheat slowly, stirring often, over low heat until hot.*

4. Ladle soup into individual soup bowls, garnishing each serving with a dollop of sour cream and a sprinkle of parsley. Serve hot.

LAMB STUFFED WITH ROASTED GARLIC AND SPINACH

Makes 8 servings

There are few main courses more festive than a beautifully browned roast stuffed with a savory filling. Buy an 8-pound leg of lamb and have the butcher bone and trim it into a boneless roast of about 5 pounds, trimming away almost all of the fat on the outside of the leg. Have the lamb butterflied to make the roast about 14 inches wide when opened. Ask the butcher to saw the bones into large pieces for the sauce.

Sauce Base

2 pounds lamb bones, sawed into pieces about 4 inches long

1 medium onion, quartered

1 medium carrot, coarsely chopped

1 celery rib, coarsely chopped

4 cups water

1 cup dry red wine

3 parsley sprigs

$\frac{1}{2}$ teaspoon dried thyme

2 garlic cloves, crushed

1 bay leaf

$\frac{1}{4}$ teaspoon whole peppercorns

Stuffing

1 head garlic, separated into unpeeled
   cloves (about 12 plump cloves)
3 tablespoons olive oil, divided
$\frac{1}{4}$ cup pine nuts
1 medium onion, finely chopped
2 (10-ounce) packages frozen chopped
   spinach, thawed and squeezed well to
   remove excess moisture
$\frac{1}{2}$ cup dried unseasoned bread crumbs
$\frac{1}{2}$ cup freshly grated Parmesan cheese
2 large eggs, beaten
1 tablespoon chopped fresh rosemary, or
   $1\frac{1}{2}$ teaspoons crumbled dried
$\frac{1}{2}$ teaspoon salt
$\frac{1}{4}$ teaspoon freshly ground pepper
$\frac{1}{8}$ teaspoon grated nutmeg

1 (5-pound) trimmed boneless leg of lamb,
   butterflied
1 tablespoon olive oil
$\frac{1}{2}$ teaspoon salt
$\frac{1}{4}$ teaspoon freshly ground pepper

1. Make the sauce base: Position a rack in top third of oven and preheat to 450°F. Place lamb bones in a large baking pan and bake until beginning to brown, about 30 minutes. Add onion, carrot, and celery and continue baking until bones are deeply browned, about 30 additional minutes. Transfer bones and vegetables to a medium saucepan and discard fat in pan.

2. Place pan on top of stove (over 2 burners, if necessary) and heat over medium-high heat. Add ½ cup water to pan and scrape up browned bits on bottom of pan with wooden spoon. Pour into saucepan with bones. Add red wine and remaining 3½ cups water. Bring to a boil over high heat, skimming off any foam rising to surface. Reduce heat to low. Add parsley, thyme, garlic, bay leaf, and peppercorns. Simmer gen-

tly until reduced to about 3½ cups, 2 to 2½ hours. Strain sauce base into a medium bowl. *The sauce base can be prepared up to 1 day ahead, cooled, covered, and refrigerated.*

3. Make the stuffing: Reduce oven to 400°F. In a small bowl, toss garlic cloves with 1 tablespoon of the oil. Place in center of a 12-inch square of aluminum foil and fold to enclose tightly. Place foil packet on a baking sheet and bake until garlic is tender, about 20 minutes. Remove garlic from foil and cool until easy to handle. Using a small, sharp knife, peel garlic, leaving cloves as whole as possible; set aside.

4. In a dry, medium skillet over medium heat, cook pine nuts, stirring often, until toasted, about 3 minutes. Transfer pine nuts to a plate and set aside.

5. In same skillet, heat remaining oil over medium heat. Add onion and cook until softened, about 5 minutes. Transfer to a medium bowl and add garlic cloves, pine nuts, spinach, bread crumbs, Parmesan cheese, eggs, rosemary, salt, pepper, and nutmeg; mix well. *The stuffing can be prepared up to 1 day ahead, without the eggs, cooled, covered, and refrigerated. Before proceeding, stir in beaten eggs.*

6. Open up lamb roast, outside down, on a work surface. Spread spinach filling evenly on lamb roast, leaving a 1-inch border all around. Starting at a short end, roll up roast and tie crosswise and lengthwise with kitchen twine. Brush with remaining olive oil and sprinkle with salt and pepper. *The roast can be prepared up to 4 hours ahead of baking, covered with plastic wrap, and refrigerated.*

7. Preheat oven to 450°F. Place roast on a rack in a roasting pan. Roast for 10 minutes. Reduce heat to 350°F. and continue roasting until a meat thermometer inserted in the center of the roast reads 130°F. for medium-rare meat, about 2¼ hours. Transfer the roast to a serving platter and let stand in a warm place for about 15 minutes before carving.

8. Discard all fat in pan. Place pan on top of stove (over 2 burners, if necessary) and pour in sauce base. Bring to a boil over high heat, scraping up browned bits on bottom of pan with a wooden spoon. Boil until sauce is thickened and reduced to about 1½ cups, 8 to 10 minutes. Keep warm until ready to serve.

9. Discard string from roast. Using a long, sharp knife, cut crosswise into thick slices. Pour the sauce into a warmed sauceboat. Serve immediately, drizzling a few spoonfuls of sauce over each serving.

MEDITERRANEAN VEGETABLE AND POTATO GRATIN

Makes 8 servings

This is my kind of cooking—an easy, colorful and flavorful dish that serves a dual purpose as vegetable and starch side dish. It's so delicious I often serve it as a vegetarian main course at simple suppers. I use a 12-by-3-inch round glazed earthenware dish, which is an inexpensive, versatile utensil sold in most kitchenware shops. It is just the right size for the large amount of vegetables, and the earthenware surface helps crisp the vegetables nicely. Lacking a large earthenware dish, you can put the vegetables in two 9-by-13-inch glass baking dishes. This recipe is easiest to make if you have a second oven, but I give instructions on how to prepare it in the oven along with the roast, if you wish. As an alternative, it can be roasted before you cook the lamb and then reheated.

1 medium eggplant (about 1 pound), cut into 1-inch cubes

3 teaspoons salt, divided

1½ pounds baking potatoes, peeled and cut into ¼-inch-thick rounds

1 pound ripe plum tomatoes, cut into ½-inch rounds, or 1 (16-ounce) can peeled tomatoes, drained and coarsely chopped

3 medium zucchini, cut into 1-inch lengths

2 large sweet red peppers, seeded and cut into 1-inch-wide strips

1 large red onion, cut into ⅓-inch-wide half-moons

4 garlic cloves, minced

½ cup extra-virgin olive oil

1 tablespoon chopped fresh thyme leaves, or 1½ teaspoons dried

¼ teaspoon freshly ground pepper

1. In a colander, toss eggplant with 1½ teaspoons salt. Let stand for at least 30 minutes and up to 2 hours. Rinse well with cold water and pat dry with paper towels.

2. Position a rack in the upper third of the oven and preheat oven to 350°F. Lightly oil a 12-by-3-inch round earthenware baking dish, or two 9-by-13-inch glass baking dishes. In a large bowl, combine eggplant, potatoes, tomatoes, zucchini, red peppers, onion, and garlic. Add olive oil, thyme, remaining 1½ teaspoons salt, and pepper and toss well. Transfer to the prepared baking dish(es.) *The gratin can be prepared, without the potatoes, up to 4 hours before baking, covered, and stored at room temperature. Keep the peeled potatoes in a large bowl of cold water. Just before baking, slice the potatoes and toss with the vegetables.*

3. Bake, stirring occasionally, until the potatoes are just tender and the gratin is lightly browned, about 1

hour, 45 minutes. Increase the heat to 450°, and bake until the edges of the vegetables are lightly browned, about 15 minutes. Cover loosely with foil and let stand for 5 minutes and up to 15 minutes before serving. *The gratin is best served soon after roasting, but it can be roasted up to 3 hours ahead, covered loosely with foil, and stored at room temperature. While the lamb roast is standing before carving, reheat the gratin in a 450°F. oven, covered loosely with the foil, until heated through, about 15 minutes.*

Note: If baking with the lamb, place gratin in lower third of oven on lowest rack. Place lamb on the next highest rack. Bake both at 450°F. for 10 minutes. Reduce temperature to 350°. Continue baking, occasionally stirring gratin, until potatoes are tender and lamb is cooked to desired temperature, about 2 hours. Remove

lamb from oven and cover loosely with foil to keep warm. Meanwhile, position broiler rack 6 inches from the source of heat and preheat broiler. Broil gratin until the tips of the vegetables are lightly browned, about 3 minutes.

WHITE CHOCOLATE GIFT BOX CAKE

Makes 8 to 10 servings

An absolutely showstopping cake! The flavor and quality of the white chocolate is very important to the success of this cake. A high-quality white chocolate has a high proportion of cocoa butter; avoid white chocolates that contain hydrogenated palm or coconut oils.

Chocolate Cake

8 tablespoons (1 stick) unsalted butter
1 teaspoon vanilla extract
$\frac{1}{2}$ cup cake flour (not self-rising)
$\frac{1}{2}$ cup Dutch-process cocoa powder, such as Dröste
$\frac{1}{2}$ teaspoon salt
6 large eggs, at room temperature
1 cup sugar

Raspberry Syrup

$\frac{1}{2}$ cup sugar
$\frac{1}{2}$ cup water
3 tablespoons raspberry-flavored liqueur, such as Chambord

Chocolate Ribbon

4 ounces semisweet chocolate, finely chopped
3 tablespoons light corn syrup
Cocoa powder, for dusting

White Chocolate Frosting

2 cups heavy cream
1 pound high-quality white chocolate, finely
    chopped

$\frac{1}{2}$ pint (6 ounces) fresh raspberries
Cake writing gel, for decoration

SPECIAL EQUIPMENT

Ravioli cutting wheel, with fluted edges
    (optional)
Metal spatula, preferably offset

1. Make the chocolate cake: Preheat oven to 350°F. Lightly butter and flour two 8-inch square cake pans (aluminum foil pans are fine). Line bottoms of pans with squares of waxed paper.

2. In a small pan, bring butter to a simmer over medium-low heat. Cook for 1 minute without brown-ing. Remove from heat and let stand 5 minutes. Skim off any foam on surface. Pour into a medium bowl, discarding any white sediment in the bottom of pan. Stir in vanilla. Sift together flour, cocoa, and salt; set aside.

3. In a large heatproof bowl, whisk eggs and sugar. Place bowl over a large saucepan of simmering water. Whisk constantly until eggs are warm to the touch and sugar is dissolved, about 2 minutes. Remove the bowl from the hot water. Using a handheld electric mixer set at high speed, beat the egg mixture until it is pale yellow and tripled in volume, about 5 minutes.

4. Sift about one-half of the flour mixture over the whipped eggs. Using a large balloon whisk or a rubber spatula, gently fold in the

flour mixture. Sift the remaining mixture over the batter and fold in. (Do this gently—don't worry if some flour remains visible.) Transfer about 1 cup of the batter to the melted butter and whisk until combined. Pour this mixture back into the batter and fold in just until combined and no flour is visible. Divide evenly between the prepared pans and smooth the tops.

5. Bake until tops of cakes spring back when pressed in centers, about 25 minutes. Cool cakes on wire racks for 5 minutes. Invert onto racks and unmold. Peel off waxed paper. Cool completely. *The cake layers can be prepared up to 3 days before serving finished cake, cooled, wrapped tightly with plastic wrap, and stored at room temperature.*

6. Make the raspberry syrup: In a small saucepan, stir sugar and water

over high heat until dissolved and boiling. Stop stirring and cook for 2 minutes. Remove from heat and stir in liqueur. Cool completely. *The raspberry syrup can be prepared up to 3 days ahead, covered and refrigerated.*

7. Make the chocolate ribbon: In the top part of a double boiler over hot, not simmering, water, melt chocolate. Remove double boiler insert from pot, and stir in corn syrup. The mixture will turn into a thick paste. Turn out onto a piece of plastic wrap and wrap tightly, forming a thick rectangle of paste as you do so. Let stand at room temperature until firm but pliable, about 2 hours. (To speed cooling, place paste in the refrigerator for 10- to 15-minute periods, but don't chill completely, or paste will turn irrevocably hard.)

8. Dust work surface with cocoa powder. Cut off one-third of paste, covering remaining paste with plastic wrap. Form into a 4-inch-long log. Using a rolling pin, roll log into a long ribbon, about 17 by 1½ inches. Using a straight edge or ruler and a fluted ravioli wheel, trim away the excess paste to make a 1-inch-wide ribbon with zigzag edges. (You may also use a small sharp knife for trimming, although you won't get the fluted edges.) Divide remaining paste in half, and repeat the procedure with each portion. To get a velvet effect, sift cocoa powder liberally over the top of ribbons. Set ribbons aside at room temperature.

9. Make the white chocolate frosting: In a medium saucepan, bring the cream to a simmer over medium heat. Place the white chocolate in a medium bowl and pour in the hot cream. Let stand for 2 minutes, then whisk until smooth.

10. Place the bowl in a larger bowl of ice water and let stand, whisking occasionally, until well chilled but not beginning to set, about 15 minutes. Remove from the water and whisk until spreadable. Do not overbeat or the frosting will turn grainy.

11. To assemble the cake, brush both sides of each layer with the syrup. Place a dab of frosting in the center of a serving platter, then center a lay-

er on top. Using a metal spatula, spread top of cake with about 1 cup frosting. Sprinkle with raspberries, pressing raspberries into frosting. Top with second layer.

12. Frost the top and sides of the cake with about two-thirds of the remaining frosting, spreading as smoothly as possible and forming sharp right angles at the corners, to give a boxlike appearance. Place cake in refrigerator until frosting is chilled and set, about 10 minutes. Frost again with remaining frosting, and

return to the refrigerator until set, an additional 10 minutes.

13. To finish the cake, cross 2 of the chocolate ribbons off-center over the cake. With a small, sharp knife, trim the ends of the ribbons where they meet the bottom of the cake. Cut a 9-inch length of the third ribbon, and bring the ends together to form a loop. Pinch the loop in the center to form 2 smaller loops, beginning a bow. Cut a 1-inch length of ribbon, and loop it over the pinched area with the ends meeting in the back to form the center of the bow. Place the bow in the center of the crossed ribbons on top of the cake. Cut two 2-inch-long strips of ribbon and place them at angles under the bow. Using the writing gel, decorate the top of the cake with desired inscription. *The finished, wrapped cake can be prepared up to 1 day ahead, loose-*

ly but completely wrapped in a few layers of plastic wrap to keep out unwanted refrigerator odors. Insert a couple of toothpicks in the top of cake so the wrap doesn't touch the inscription.

14. Remove the cake from the refrigerator 1 hour before serving. Use a long, sharp knife to cut the cake crosswise into 2 rectangles. Cut each rectangle vertically into thick slices.